The
Sovereignty
of
God

Andrew Wommack

Published by Andrew Wommack Ministries, Inc.

Woodland Park, CO 80863

ISBN 13 TP: 978-1-59548-755-1

For Worldwide Distribution, Printed in the USA

1 2 3 4 5 6 / 28 27 26 25

Contents

Would you like to get more out of this teaching?

Scan the QR code to access this teaching in video or audio formats to help you dive even deeper as you study.

Accessing the teaching this way will help you get even more out of this booklet.

awmi.net/browse

Is God Sovereign?

I believe God is absolutely sovereign! There is no one higher or greater. The Lord God Almighty is the top of the food chain. No one gives Him directions. He is self-existent and the Creator of all that exists. Amen! End of story. There is no debating this point.

But what does sovereign mean? That's where my problem with the popular teaching on the sovereignty of God exists. If you use the dictionary definition of sovereign which is, "a supreme ruler, monarch, or first in order or rank,"[1] I agree with that completely.

However, there is a religious definition of the word sovereign which you won't find in any dictionary. That

---

[1] Oxford English Dictionary, s.v. "sovereign," accessed March 6, 2025, https://www.oed.com/dictionary/sovereign_n?tab=meaning_and_use#21519750

religious definition is that God controls everything, and nothing can happen without Him first approving it. All sickness and disease, poverty, hurt and pain, and every evil work originates with or has to be approved by God. That is absolutely wrong and contrary to what the Bible teaches.

I have a BIG problem with that religious teaching on the sovereignty of God. In my opinion, it is the worst doctrine in the body of Christ today.

There are many reasons I'm so passionate about this, but one big reason is that this teaching makes people passive. If God truly controls everything, then what's the incentive to seek the Lord, pray, resist the devil, or do anything? If that teaching is true, then whatever we do doesn't matter. God's will is going to come to pass regardless of what we do. That defies logic and everything the Word of God teaches.

James 4:7 says,

Submit yourselves therefore to God. Resist the devil, and he will flee from you.

This verse reveals there are things from God which we submit to and there are things from the devil that we resist. There would be no purpose for this verse if God just sovereignly controlled everything. If God's will automatically came to pass regardless of what we do, why submit to God and why resist the devil? Just live however you want to, and whatever the Lord wants will automatically happen.

If a person really believed that the Lord is the one who made them sick, they would be resisting God's will if they went to the doctor or took medicine. To be consistent in their beliefs, they should just let the sickness or disease run its course and suffer like God intended them to suffer. Of course, I don't believe that, and you shouldn't either.

That wrong teaching about the sovereignty of God takes away all motive for seeking the Lord. That extreme sovereignty teaching says whatever happens was destined to happen, regardless of what we do. That's absurd.

As a whole, people blame God for whatever happens. They even write into their contracts that you are insured for everything except "acts of God," like tornados, hurricanes, fires, floods, and earthquakes. They pray for healing, but if the person dies, they say it must have been their time. They couldn't have died if it wasn't the Lord's will.

I watched a TV interview where a woman recounted how she and her daughter were abducted, taken to a remote place, raped, and shot in the back of the head. The daughter died, but the mother survived and was on this Christian program saying the Lord willed all of this. She was so much closer to the Lord because of what happened, so she believed it couldn't have happened if it wasn't the Lord's will.

She blamed God for rape and murder! That's a lie! That is blasphemy in my book (the Bible). Blasphemy is attributing the works of God to the devil and vice versa (Mark 3:28-30). It's calling the good that God does evil, and the evil the devil does good (Isaiah 5:20). That's what the modern sovereignty of God teaching does.

Evil Is Not from God

Deuteronomy 28 clearly states what the Lord calls a blessing and what He calls a curse. The first fourteen verses list the blessings, and verses fifteen through sixty-eight list the curses. Sickness, poverty, fear, and various types of oppression are on the curses side of that list. Health, victory over our enemies, abundant crops, and such prosperity that we would lend and never have to borrow are on the blessings side. The Lord called the opposite of the blessings, curses. We should accept His evaluation of what's good and bad and reject the religious lie that He is the author of our tragedies.

Those who promote sickness, poverty, and all kinds of suffering are opposing God's values. They are attributing the works of the devil to God. That's wrong on every level. If our enemy can get us to embrace what he is doing as being the work of God, we'll submit to it, thereby voiding God's command in James 4:7 to resist the devil.

Throughout this teaching, I'll be referring to "religion" in a negative way. That's because I define religion as man's opinion about God and His requirements for righteousness. Christianity isn't religion in that sense. Christianity is God's revelation of Himself to us through the Bible and is usually the opposite of what "religion" teaches.

I believe one of the reasons "religion" promotes this wrong sovereignty of God doctrine is because it's an excuse for our ignorance or lack of power. Instead of accepting responsibility when things go wrong, they just push it off on God with statements like, "It must have been His will."

At the beginning of my ministry, I prayed for a four-year-old boy who died in my arms. I did everything I knew to do, but we didn't see him come back to life. The parents asked me to perform his funeral, and I was at a loss for what to say that could comfort them. I was really tempted to blame his death on the Lord and just say, "The Lord works in mysterious ways. It must have been His will."

Instead, I told them the truth. I said, "I don't know why he wasn't healed, but it wasn't because the Lord willed it. Either I missed it, or you missed it, or maybe we just don't know enough to see victory in this situation." But I told them that God didn't kill their child. I didn't know what the problem was, but I wasn't going to let what I didn't know keep me from acting on what I did know.

In a few months, the mother explained to me that her son was born prematurely in a taxi before they got to a hospital. There were complications; he was mentally disabled and his immune system didn't work. The doctors told her if he ever got a cold, he would have no resistance and would probably die from it. She realized those words had instilled fear in her and she had been dreading that day for four years. When he got sick, all that fear that had been incubating in her for all those years simply overwhelmed her faith.

She thanked me for telling her the truth instead of just saying something that would have comforted her in the short term. She determined she would not let that happen again. The doctors said that because she was petite, if she had more children, they would have to be delivered by cesarean section. She didn't want that, so she had her other three children at home by natural childbirth. As each child graduated from high school, she sent me a picture of them in their caps and gowns with a thank you note for telling her the truth.

At the time of that funeral, I was sorely tempted to tell them God took their child. That would have soothed them temporarily and gotten me off the hook for any failure on my part, but it wasn't the truth. Jesus said it's the truth that makes us free (John 8:32). The truth is that God is a good God and isn't the author of sickness, poverty, hurt, pain, and death (Heb. 2:15).

All kinds of things are taking place in this fallen world that are not caused by God. He doesn't cause the evil, nor does He allow it. All the tragedy in the human race comes from us selling out to the devil and giving him control.

James 4:1 says,

From whence come wars and fightings among you? come they *not hence,* even *of your lusts that war in your members?*

That verse clearly states that wars don't come from God. It's our own lust that results in the conflict we see in the world today. Although there are justifiable wars where nations defend themselves from the aggression of evil, those wars still originate because some person or nation was motivated by their own evil desires.

God's Will Is Not Automatic

Here is a truth that should convince anyone who lets the Bible be the foundation of their beliefs. The Lord doesn't just sovereignly make His will come to pass. Second Peter 3:9 says,

The Lord is not slack concerning his promise, as some men count slackness; but is longsuffering to us-ward, not willing that any should perish, but that all should come to repentance.

That's as clear as the Lord can make it. It is not God's will for any to perish, but they do. Jesus even said that more would enter by the broad gate unto destruction than by the narrow gate that leads to everlasting life (Matt. 7:13-14). Yet this verse clearly states that it's the Lord's will for everyone to come to salvation. **This shows that God's will does not sovereignly (independently of man) come to pass.**

That's why the angel in Acts 10 told Cornelius to send for Peter to come and preach the Gospel to him. I'm sure the angel knew the Gospel better than Peter did. But the angel didn't have the authority to preach the Gospel. The Lord gave that authority to His church. If people aren't hearing the Gospel, it's not God's fault. It's the fault of His body, which is supposed to be fulfilling the great commission of Matthew 28:19-20.

The children of Israel are another example. The Lord definitely brought them out of Egypt to bring them into the Promised Land. It wasn't God's will for them to die in the wilderness, but the whole older generation perished. That wasn't God's plan for them. The Lord had only good plans for them with a glorious future (Jer. 29:11). Hebrews 3:19 confirms this by saying they didn't enter in because of unbelief. God's plans for us don't come to pass sovereignly. We have to cooperate with God through faith to obtain His goodness. By choosing not to believe God, they doomed themselves to death in the desert.

The prophet Jonah is also an example. The Lord told him to go to Ninevah and warn them of God's impending judgment. Jonah didn't want to do it because the Ninevites were Israel's enemies. Jonah wanted them to be judged so they wouldn't be a threat to Israel anymore. So, he boarded a ship and headed in the opposite direction. However, he couldn't escape from the Lord.

The Lord sent a violent storm, and the sailors threw him overboard to appease God's wrath. God prepared a great fish that swallowed Jonah, and after three days and nights, the fish spit him out on dry land. He finally headed for Ninevah, probably bleached white from gastric juices with seaweed around his neck, to finally do what the Lord told him to do.

Jonah recorded the prayer he prayed in the total darkness of the fish's belly. Jonah said,

They that observe lying vanities forsake their own mercy.

Jonah 2:8

It wasn't God's original plan to have Jonah swallowed by a fish. God had a plan of mercy for Jonah and the Ninevites. It was Jonah that chose his course of rebellion that could have resulted in his death. But even in his disobedience, the Lord was merciful and gave him another chance. It was Jonah's own rebellion that made him "fish bait." It's the same thing with us.

The Lord gives us choices. That's why He told us to choose life in Deuteronomy 30:19.

I call heaven and earth to record this day against you, that I have set before you life and death, blessing and cursing: therefore choose life, that both thou and thy seed may live:

The Lord gives us the choice between life and death, blessing and cursing. There would be no choice to it if He just sovereignly forced His will upon us. No! We have a choice. It should be a "no-brainer" between life and death or blessing and cursing. But just in case anyone doesn't know which choice to make, He gave us the answer. He said, "choose life."

There are many who reject the existence of God because of all the suffering they see in the world, and the extreme sovereignty of God teaching fuels their reasonings. If there was a God, why would He let things like the Holocaust take place? How could He stand by and watch people suffer with sickness and disease? What about all the innocent children that are being trafficked and dying of hunger? Why doesn't He do something?

These are valid questions that need to be answered, but blaming God for all this suffering is not the right answer. It's not God who is letting all these terrible things happen. We have an enemy who only comes to steal, kill, and destroy (John 10:10). The devil is the one who sets the whole course of this world on fire

(James 3:6), and our original parents in the Garden of Eden are the ones who enabled him to do it.

Mankind's Sovereignty

The Lord created the universe, and as Creator, everything belonged to Him and was originally under His dominion. But Psalm 115:16 says,

The heaven, even the heavens, are the Lord's: but the earth hath he given to the children of men.

He gave the earth to the children of men. That means that even though the Lord is Creator, and therefore, owner, He gave the dominion (control-management) of the earth to man. The Lord doesn't directly control everything that takes place on earth. That's our job. He only exerts His influence through mankind.

Genesis 1:26-28 says,

*And God said, Let us make man in our image, after our likeness: and let them have **dominion***

over the fish of the sea, and over the fowl of the air, and over the cattle, and over all the earth, and over every creeping thing that creepeth upon the earth. So God created man in his own *image, in the image of God created he him; male and female created he them. And God blessed them, and God said unto them, Be fruitful, and multiply, and replenish the earth, and subdue it: and have **dominion** over the fish of the sea, and over the fowl of the air, and over every living thing that moveth upon the earth.* (emphasis added)

Notice that the Lord said twice in these verses that mankind was to have dominion over all animals and everything that moves upon the earth. By saying this, the Lord limited His sovereignty over the earth. He delegated that power to man. The Lord made mankind sovereign over the earth.

Psalm 89:34 says,

My covenant will I not break, nor alter the thing that is gone out of my lips.

Combine that verse with Hebrews 6:18, which says it is impossible for God to lie, and it's easy to see that the Lord could not just step in and fix everything when Adam and Eve sinned and plunged the whole human race into chaos. The Lord had given His word that mankind had control of this earth. It was ours to do with as we pleased. He would not break His word.

This is hard for us to understand because we don't have as much integrity as the Lord. Psalm 15:4 says that a godly person will swear to his own hurt and not change, but most people won't stand by their word if it works to their disadvantage. Even contracts aren't binding to many people if they have enough money to hire a good "shyster" lawyer.

But God can't lie, and He will not alter what He has said regardless of the consequences. Whatever comes out of the Lord's mouth is a covenant. Again, Psalm 89:34 says,

My covenant will I not break, nor alter the thing that is gone out of my lips.

Hebrews 1:3 says,

Who being the brightness of his *glory, and the express image of his person, and upholding all things by the word of his power, when he had by himself purged our sins, sat down on the right hand of the Majesty on high;*

This verse is speaking of Jesus, and it reveals that Jesus holds all things together by the word of His power. That's profound. Combine that truth with Colossians 1:16-17 which says,

For by him were all things created, that are in heaven, and that are in earth, visible and invisible, whether they be *thrones, or dominions, or principalities, or powers: all things were created by him, and for him: And he is before all things, and by him all things consist.*

Jesus created everything that was created, and everything He created is held together by the integrity of His word. If He ever broke His word, the universe would fly apart.

Psalm 138:2 says,

...for thou hast magnified thy word above all thy name.

Think of what this is saying. God's word is magnified more than His name because a man's name is no better than his word. The name of Jesus is a strong tower. At the name of Jesus, every knee is going to bow, and every tongue will confess that Jesus is Lord (Phil. 2:9-11). Yet the Lord has magnified His word greater than His name. If the Lord didn't keep His word, His name would be powerless.

If you understand this, then it's easy to see why the Lord could not just intervene in the affairs of men after Adam committed high treason and turned the control of the earth over to Satan. God had given His word. God cannot lie, so He could not break His oath to Adam that the earth was his to do with as he pleased.

Of course, the Lord never wanted us to yield that authority and dominion to the devil. That was not His will, but He didn't force His will upon Adam and Eve. He gave them a choice, and they chose poorly.

The Lord had given His word to Adam and Eve that they were in control. He would not break His word in order to right their wrong. God cannot lie. His integrity would not allow Him to go back on the promise that He gave them, even with the terrible results that it produced.

Imagine that I owned a farm and gave it to my son with no strings attached. It was his to do with as he pleased. Then, a crook comes by and deceives him into signing the whole farm over to him. What could I do? It was all legal. Although it was not what I intended, I had given my word and signed the papers to my son, and he had signed the title deed over to this thief. I would be bound by the law.

The only alternative I would have under the law would be to buy the farm back from the thief and, once again, return it to my son. However, to safeguard the farm, I would make the ownership a joint owner-ship between my son and me. That would return the delegated control of the farm to my son but would protect it from any charlatan ever taking it away again. Even if my son was deceived again, I would never agree with him and sign the deed over to someone else.

In a similar fashion, the Lord gave dominion over the earth to mankind, and mankind gave his dominion over the earth to Satan. Because it's impossible for God to lie, He would have been unjust to just step in and destroy Satan. He had the power to do that but not the authority. He had given authority over the earth to man, and man had willfully surrendered it to Satan. Our just God cannot break a covenant that has gone out of His lips (Ps. 89:34).

So, the Lord bought or redeemed mankind back to Himself by becoming a man and paying the sin debt that we owed. Romans 6:23 says the wages of sin is death. There was a debt that had to be paid, and Jesus paid that debt in full. Through His sacrifice, Jesus redeemed (bought back) mankind and gained back all the authority and dominion we foolishly gave away.

The Lord gave authority over the earth to mankind (Ps. 115:16); however, He still rules in the heavens. Through Jesus' death and resurrection, the Lord regained authority over the earth, and thus Jesus said in Matthew 28:18,

> *…All power is given unto me in heaven and in earth.*

The Lord bought back the earth through Jesus, and now He shares that authority and power with His body, the church (Eph. 1:18-23). Because it's a joint heirship (Rom. 8:17), mankind will never be able to "give away the farm" again. A joint checking account requires two signatures in order to be valid. Likewise, a joint heirship requires both parties to consent before any transaction goes into effect.

Even if we consent to the lies of the devil, our Lord Jesus never will. Therefore, our inheritance is secure regardless of what deception we submit to. We give the devil an inroad into our lives when we yield to him, but our inheritance is not subject to our mistakes. Our salvation is safe because we are joint heirs with Jesus.

In the Garden of Eden, Adam and Eve weren't joint heirs with God. They had absolute, sovereign dominion over the earth. Satan couldn't force them to disobey God. He had no authority. That's why he had to choose the most subtle (cunning or crafty) animal the Lord had created (Gen. 3:1). He didn't get an elephant to put his foot on Eve's head and say, "Eat the forbidden fruit or I'll squash your head like a melon," or a lion to say, "Eat or I'll tear you limb from limb." The devil didn't have authority over the earth at that time. Adam and Eve were the sole rulers.

All the devil could do was lie to them and tempt them to disobey the Lord. He couldn't do anything without their consent and cooperation. They were in charge. But through yielding to the devil's lies, they are the ones who empowered Satan with the dominion and power that the Lord intended mankind to have.

Romans 6:16 says,

Know ye not, that to whom ye yield yourselves servants to obey, his servants ye are to whom ye

*obey; whether of sin unto death, or of obedience
unto righteousness?*

That verse is simply saying that whoever we obey has dominion over us. Through yielding to the devil, Adam and Eve gave control of the earth, which God had given to them (Ps. 115:16), to Satan. That's when Satan became the god of this world (2 Cor. 4:4).

Since the Lord had sworn to man that the earth was his and he could do with it as he wished, the Lord would have been unjust to destroy Satan and put things back to the way He wanted it to be. Adam and Eve were complicit in Satan's rebellion. If the Lord judged Satan, He would also have to judge His children, which gave Satan this power.

In a sense, Satan used mankind as a hostage. It's like when a thief comes into a bank. There could be armed guards that have more firepower than the thief. But if the thief takes a hostage and threatens to harm them unless his demands are met, then he could escape because they don't want to harm the hostage.

Satan knew the Lord loved Adam and Eve so much that He wouldn't forsake them. So, the devil got Adam and Eve to give him the deed to the earth willfully, and if the Lord wanted to destroy Satan, He would have to destroy the hostage, too. They willingly chose to follow the devil and his lies.

Likewise, the Lord loves us so much that He didn't want to destroy the people He created. Therefore, He allowed Satan to become the god of this world (2 Cor. 4:4). That was originally our position (Ps. 82:6). The Lord created mankind to be the absolute authority (gods) of this world. I'm not speaking of God in the divine sense, but the Lord gave total control of the earth to mankind to rule as we saw fit.

So, the devil is using the authority mankind gave him, which allowed him to be the god of this world and cause all the hurt and pain we see today. God is not the author of all the suffering we see and is only allowing it in the sense that He's upholding the integrity of His word and our free will. He allows what we allow.

If you have followed my reasoning up to this point and understand that the Lord gave unconditional dominion over the earth to mankind, then this will also answer some other questions like why did God have to become a man?

That's because in John 4:24 Jesus said,

God is a Spirit: and they that worship him must worship him in spirit and in truth.

The Lord gave dominion over the earth to human beings with physical bodies. Since God is a Spirit, He didn't have a physical body and authority in the earth. Neither did the devil. He's a spiritual being, too. That's why Satan had to use a talking snake to interact with Adam and Eve.

In order to gain back what was lost through Adam, a physical being who had authority in the earth had to do the job. So, the Lord sought a man that He could work through to gain back what Adam gave away. That's what Ezekiel 22:30 reveals,

And I sought for a man among them, that should make up the hedge, and stand in the gap before me for the land, that I should not destroy it: but I found none.

There wasn't a single person on the earth who could redeem us because all of mankind has sinned and come short of the glory of God (Rom. 3:23). Since every naturally born person has sinned, none of us could be a spotless lamb to pay for the sins of the world. That's why Jesus had to become a man. He offered Himself as a sacrifice for our sins to pay the debt we owed.

By becoming a man, Jesus not only died in our place so we wouldn't have to suffer eternal separation from God, but that also gave Him authority in the earth so He could deal directly with the devil. In a sense, Jesus became one of the hostages without ever yielding to the devil. Therefore, Satan had no control over Him, but Jesus then had the authority to deal with the devil because He had become flesh. That put Satan in a very bad situation.

This is exactly what Jesus was referring to in John 5:26-27 when He said,

For as the Father hath life in himself; so hath he given to the Son to have life in himself; And hath given him authority to execute judgment also, because he is the Son of man.

Jesus said the reason He had authority to execute judgment in the earth was because "*he is the Son of man.*" The term "Son of God" refers to the divinity of Jesus. But the term "Son of man" refers to the human part of Him. Jesus was sinless because He was born of a virgin (Luke 1:26-27), but He did have a human body that had to grow in wisdom and stature and favor with God and man (Luke 2:52). Jesus' physical body gave Him authority in the earth just like Adam had at one time.

So, Jesus took the authority His human body gave Him and took the fight to the devil. He overcame all sickness and disease, walked on water, multiplied food supernaturally, cast out devils, and raised people from the dead. When He died, He descended into hell and took the keys of hell and death away from the devil (Rev. 1:18) and then rose to new life with all authority in heaven and in earth.

Then He turned around and gave that power and authority back to us. He is now in charge again, but He's not ruling and reigning alone. He only works through His body, the church. He does not work "sovereignly" or "independently" of His people.

God Works Through Us

Ephesians 3:20 says,

Now unto him that is able to do exceeding abundantly above all that we ask or think, according to the power that worketh in us,

People often quote the first part of that verse and say there are no limits on God. He can do so much greater than anything we can ask or think. But that's not what that verse says. It specifically limits God's ability to do great things to the power that works in us.

If there is no power working in us, God's power won't work. It's a joint heirship.

You will often hear people quote a scripture like Proverbs 21:1, which says,

> *The king's heart* is *in the hand of the Lord, as the rivers of water: he turneth it whithersoever he will.*

From this and other scriptures, like Romans 13, people think God sovereignly controls who is in power and everything they do. But look at Hosea 8:4. That verse says,

> *They have set up kings, but not by me: they have made princes, and I knew* it *not:*

That verse clearly reveals that we can put people in positions of authority without His consent. The Lord is not the one who puts despots on the throne. The god of this world works through the ungodly to steal, kill, and destroy, while Christ's body is the counterpart— the salt and light of the world. But when Christians don't do their part, it gives the devil the upper hand to work evil through those who submit to him.

The Lord exerts His power and authority through His body. If we don't let His power flow through us, we can hinder or stop His will from coming to pass.

This became personal to me on January 31, 2002, when the Lord spoke Psalm 78:41 directly to me. That verse says,

Yea, they turned back and tempted God, and limited the Holy One of Israel.

That was referring to the Israelites that came out of Egypt. The Lord told them to go in and possess the land He had given them. But they listened to the ten spies who brought up an evil report instead of Joshua and Caleb who spoke that they were well able to take the land (Num. 13). The Lord had more than enough power to overcome the giants in the land, but He could only use that power as His people yielded to Him. He had to flow through them.

When the majority of the people listened to the "Ten Spies Network" more than the word of God, they limited what God could do. That's amazing. Most people believe the Lord can do anything He wants, but that's not what this verse is saying. It says we can limit God through our unbelief.

That's what the Lord said to me through this verse. I knew what God's will for my life was, and I was doing it, but at a snail's pace. The Lord spoke directly to me that my small thinking was limiting what He was able to do through me. I've got multiple teachings that go into great detail about how I responded and what that enabled the Lord to do in and through me. But suffice it to say, that was one of the most important adjustments I've ever made in my life.

My ministry increased over one hundred times in reach during the next two decades. I've seen growth and provision that cannot be explained without giving all the glory to God. As my mother so bluntly told me as I was describing to her what the Lord had done, she said, "Andy, you know this is God." I agreed and gave all the glory to God. Then she said, "You aren't smart enough to do this." Again, there was no argument from me. It's totally supernatural what has happened since then.

The miracles I've experienced were supernatural, but they were not solely the result of divine sovereignty. I played a part. I didn't cause them, but I had to get out of my small thinking and start believing God so He would have something to work with. It was the Lord's doing, but it was according to the power that worked in me.

Every one of us has had the Lord tell us very clearly not to do something, and we did it anyway. Isn't that true? That's what the Bible calls sin. James 4:17 says,

> *Therefore to him that knoweth to do good, and doeth* it *not, to him it is sin.*

So, every one of us has knowingly disobeyed God at some time. If the Lord doesn't control us like a robot, and we are free to disobey God, what makes you think He controls everyone and everything else that way?

Someone might be thinking of Romans 8:28, which says,

And we know that all things work together for good to them that love God, to them who are the called according to his *purpose.*

This verse has been interpreted to say that everything that happens to us comes from God and is meant to accomplish something good in our lives. That's not what this verse says.

I actually heard a preacher give a testimony using this verse to justify being controlled by lust. He was so full of lust that he said during one of his sermons that he would mentally undress the women sitting before him in the congregation. He finally admitted his problem and scheduled an appointment to get some help.

As he was getting in his car to go to the appointment, he said the Lord told him, "You couldn't have this problem if I had not allowed it. If you get deliverance from this, you won't learn the lesson I'm trying to teach you." So, believing that lie, he cancelled his appointment and kept the lust. He eventually failed morally and was forced to get out of the ministry.

That wasn't the Lord who told him that He had given him lust to accomplish some redemptive purpose in his life. That was the false teaching about an extreme sovereignty of God where nothing can happen to you unless the Lord wills it or allows it. That's foolish.

I heard another preacher who had just come from conducting a funeral for a couple of teenagers. They had been drinking and were driving too fast on a slick road. They couldn't keep the car on a curve and went off the road, hitting a telephone pole. Both died in the crash, and neither one of them knew the Lord.

Yet this preacher got up and said that although we don't understand the ways of the Lord, we know the Lord works all things together for good. So, this must have been God's will to kill these two young teenagers.

I got so mad I could have spit bullets. That's not what Romans 8:28 teaches.

First of all, that verse doesn't say that everything that happens comes from the Lord. It's simply saying the Lord can take anything that happens and work it together for good, but there are qualifications on that.

The verse begins with the word "And," which is a conjunction that ties this verse to the previous verses. Romans 8:26-27 spoke about the Holy Spirit enabling us to intercede beyond our own ability with groanings that cannot be uttered. All things work together for our good *only* if we have been functioning in this supernaturally empowered intercession.

All things will only work together for our good if we 1) love the Lord and 2) are the called according to his purpose. Those are two big ifs.

This minister who had officiated the funeral of the two teenagers specifically said that they were not born again. That means they didn't meet the first requirement of loving the Lord. Everything doesn't work together for good for those who don't love the Lord. Also, you have to be called according to His purpose. What was the purpose of the Lord? First John 3:8 says,

...For this purpose the Son of God was manifested, that he might destroy the works of the devil.

These two teenagers weren't living to destroy the works of the devil. They were going against what their parents had probably told them and the law that required them not to drink and drive. They weren't resisting the devil. They were cooperating with him by their actions, and it cost them their lives, physically and spiritually.

So, putting all of this together, Romans 8:28 is saying that for those who are allowing the Holy Spirit to intercede through them, *and* who love the Lord, *and* who are out to destroy the works of the devil, then, and only then, can all things work together for good.

An example of this is when my son died. My oldest son called me at 4:15 a.m. and told me that my youngest son had died. I asked what had happened and then told him not to let anyone touch him until I got there. My wife and I got up, and it took us one hour and fifteen minutes to drive into Colorado Springs to where my son was.

We didn't have cell phones at that time, so we didn't know until we got to the hospital what the outcome would be. But immediately, we spoke our faith and rebuked this death sentence over our son. As we were driving into town, we started having all the thoughts and emotions that anyone would have in that situation. But we let the Holy Spirit intercede through us by speaking in tongues. We also loved the Lord with all of our hearts, not only at that moment because our backs were against the wall, but we were deeply in love with the Lord at all times.

In fact, one of the things I did during that drive into town was start praising the Lord and telling Him I would love Him regardless of the outcome. I knew He wasn't the one who killed my son, and I would not blame Him if he didn't come back to life. My son died because of his own actions, not God's. We also let loose on the devil and told him where he could go.

When we arrived at the hospital, my oldest son met us at the door and said he didn't know what happened, but just a few minutes after he called me, my son just sat up and started talking. He had been dead for over four hours. He was already in a cooler in the hospital morgue, stripped naked, with a toe tag on. Yet, he rose up and started talking with no brain damage. That was over twenty-four years ago at this writing, and I have a beautiful granddaughter through him who has the unique honor of being born one year after her father died. Praise the Lord!

Since we allowed the Holy Spirit to intercede through us, and because we loved God and knew how to take our authority and rebuke the devil, the Lord worked this terrible situation out for good. I've been able to rub the devil's nose in his defeat ever since, and it has inspired hope in countless people.

But that wouldn't have happened if we submitted to his death, thinking that it couldn't happen unless the Lord wanted it to happen. No, the resurrection happened because we knew the truth and resisted what the devil was trying to do to kill our son. Through the power of faith working in us, the Lord was able to do exceedingly abundantly above all we could ask or think. Thank you, Jesus.

A person who believes the Lord is the one who brings tragedy into their lives can't truly resist the devil, because according to their way of thinking, they would be resisting God. If God is the author of the problem, then resisting the problem would be resisting God. No one in their right mind would do that.

At the beginning of my walk with the Lord, I was taught that the Lord sovereignly controlled everything that happened. My dad died when I had just turned twelve years old. My Baptist pastor told me that it was the Lord's will. He said God needed my dad in heaven more than I needed him. I was only twelve, but I was smart enough to know that wasn't true. However, I pretty much submitted to the doctrine that the Lord controls everything that happens, even (or especially) bad things.

Right after I had my amazing encounter with the Lord on March 23, 1968, I went to a conference where a minister was saying that Satan is God's "messenger boy." This minister described the devil as a dog on a leash and he could only go as far as the Lord would allow him to go. So, if the devil was attacking us, God was allowing it for some redemptive purpose.

He gave an example of a young high school boy who wanted to be a witness to his football buddies, but he was just too shy to speak out. So, he asked the Lord to give him cancer so he could show his friends he wasn't afraid to die. The next morning, he woke up with leukemia. He used his lack of fear of death to testify to his friends, and at his funeral, four people were born again.

I brought that teaching back and shared it with a girlfriend of mine. She prayed the same prayer, and the next morning, she woke up with leukemia, just like the boy in the sermon. We tried to believe the Lord for healing, even having the pastor anoint her with oil in the name of the Lord (James 5:14-15). But she also died, and at her funeral, four people received the Lord.

That wasn't the Lord answering their prayers and giving them cancer. That was the devil who took advantage of our wrong believing. It's the devil that comes to steal, kill, and destroy. Jesus came to give us abundant life (John 10:10). Satan is going about seeking whom he may devour (1 Pet. 5:8), and those who submit to him—because of wrong doctrine about God's sovereignty—are exactly the tasty meal he is looking for.

A man brought his twelve-year-old quadriplegic daughter to one of my meetings. As I was teaching on this very issue of sovereignty, he got so mad that he left my meeting. A friend asked him to stay and talk to me after the meeting which he did. He was standing behind his daughter, who was in a wheelchair, and I was facing her. He shared scriptures with me that he thought made the Lord responsible for his daughter being like that from birth. I shared with him many of the scriptures I've shared in this booklet that the Lord isn't the one who causes these tragedies.

I understood that the only way the father had been able to cope with this terrible situation was to think that God, in His superior wisdom, knew this was best. I was removing his coping mechanism by saying that the Lord didn't do this to his daughter, and he was hopping mad. I figured I had nothing to lose so I did something I would only do if the Lord directed me to do it.

I asked him what kind of father he was that he wanted his daughter to be like that. That nearly pushed him over the edge. If he hadn't been behind the wheelchair, I think he would have come after me. He said he loved his daughter and would do anything to see her healed and normal. If he could, he would become like her so she could be like him. Then I told him, "And you think God Almighty loves her less than you do." I went on to tell him that's exactly what Jesus did for us. He became like us so we could be like Him (2 Cor. 5:21).

That totally stopped him in his tracks. He finally understood that a loving God would never make someone quadriplegic. Our loving heavenly Father isn't the one causing all the evil in this world. Jesus came to redeem us out from under the authority of the devil, and for those who walk in the authority He gave back to us, we can reverse the suffering the devil brings.

If an imperfect person would not "bless" their child with cancer, poverty, depression, or any other evil thing, then how can anyone think that our God, who loved us so much that He was willing to become a man and die in our place, loves us less. That's what Luke 11:11-13 says,

If a son shall ask bread of any of you that is a father, will he give him a stone? or if he ask a fish, will he for a fish give him a serpent? Or if he shall ask an egg, will he offer him a scorpion? If ye then, being evil, know how to give good gifts unto your children: how much more shall your heavenly Father give the Holy Spirit to them that ask him?

God is a good God who only has good things for those who will believe and receive. He is not the one who is causing or allowing tragedy in our lives. Faith works by love, and love doesn't give sickness, poverty, and all types of hurt and pain to people.

Conclusion

Religion has taught through this incorrect sovereignty of God doctrine that our loving God is the perpetrator of all the evil in this life. If I went around causing death and destruction, as God is accused of doing, there isn't a civilized nation on this earth that wouldn't justifiably arrest and punish me.

Blaming God for all the evil in this world has turned many people away from the Lord. And even those who keep their faith in the Lord may become angry and bitter toward Him because they think He could have kept their loved one alive, preserved their marriage, or intervened in some other way if He wanted to. That's not the case. Anyone who is angry with the Lord because of bad things that have happened to them or those they love does not understand the truths I've shared in this booklet.

The Lord provided a way to redeem us back to His original plan through the atonement of Jesus. Those who reject Jesus are rejecting God's deliverance (Acts 4:12) and purchasing to themselves damnation. They are still under the dominion of the god of this world and don't have any hope of living above his power (Eph. 2:12).

Even among those of us who accept Jesus and become joint heirs with Him of this glorious salvation, we still have a part to play. We have to let the power of truth and faith work in us for Him to work through us.

This teaching on the sovereignty of God still leaves questions. I have a 176-page book entitled *The War is Over*, which deals with things like why the Lord struck people with plagues and sickness under the Old Covenant. None of those instances were blessings; they were all expressions of God's judgment. Under our new and better covenant (Heb. 8:6), we have been redeemed from these curses because Jesus became a curse for us (Gal. 3:13). God's war against our sin is over because Jesus became sin for us and made us the righteousness of God (2 Cor. 5:21).

The book of Job has also been used incorrectly to preach the extreme sovereignty of God. I don't have time in this booklet to deal with what was really going on in that situation. I have over 650 footnotes in my *Living Commentary* that explain it. I encourage you to get these resources and the ones listed at the end of this booklet.

I hope this brief teaching has shed some light on the truth about the sovereignty of God doctrine and why God is not to blame when bad things happen. The idea that God sovereignly controls everything, and nothing happens without His direct approval, is wrong and contradicts what the Bible teaches. Every good and perfect gift comes from God. The devil is the one who steals, kills, and destroys. We have a choice: who will we cooperate with? If we put our faith in God and allow His power to work through us, we will experience His will for our lives—abundant life.

FURTHER STUDY

If you enjoyed this booklet and would like to learn more about some of the things I've shared, I suggest my teachings:

1. *The Authority of the Believer*
2. *Don't Limit God*
3. *My Appointment with God*
4. *The True Nature of God*
5. *The War is Over*

Plus 200,000 hours of free teaching on our website.

These teachings are available for free at **awmi.net**, or they can be purchased at **awmi.net/store**.

Go deeper in your relationship with God by browsing all of Andrew's free teachings.

Receive Jesus as Your Savior

Choosing to receive Jesus Christ as your Lord and Savior is the most important decision you'll ever make!

God's Word promises, *"That if thou shalt confess with thy mouth the Lord Jesus, and shalt believe in thine heart that God hath raised him from the dead, thou shalt be saved. For with the heart man believeth unto righteousness; and with the mouth confession is made unto salvation"* (Rom. 10:9–10). *"For whosoever shall call upon the name of the Lord shall be saved"* (Rom. 10:13). By His grace, God has already done everything to provide salvation. Your part is simply to believe and receive.

Pray out loud: "Jesus, I acknowledge that I've sinned and need to receive what you did for the forgiveness of my sins. I confess that You are my Lord and Savior. I believe in my heart that God raised You from the dead. By faith in Your Word, I receive salvation now. Thank You for saving me."

The very moment you commit your life to Jesus Christ, the truth of His Word instantly comes to pass in your spirit. Now that you're born again, there's a brand-new you!

Please contact us and let us know that you've prayed to receive Jesus as your Savior. We'd like to send you some free materials to help you on your new journey. Call our Helpline: **719-635-1111** (available 24 hours a day, seven days a week) to speak to a staff member who is here to help you understand and grow in your new relationship with the Lord.

Welcome to your new life!

Receive the Holy Spirit

As His child, your loving heavenly Father wants to give you the supernatural power you need to live a new life. *"For every one that asketh receiveth; and he that seeketh findeth; and to him that knocketh it shall be opened... how much more shall* your *heavenly Father give the Holy Spirit to them that ask him?"* (Luke 11:10–13).

All you have to do is ask, believe, and receive! Pray this: "Father, I recognize my need for Your power to live a new life. Please fill me with Your Holy Spirit. By faith, I receive it right now. Thank You for baptizing me. Holy Spirit, You are welcome in my life."

Some syllables from a language you don't recognize will rise up from your heart to your mouth (1 Cor. 14:14). As you speak them out loud by faith, you're releasing God's power from within and building yourself up in the spirit (1 Cor. 14:4). You can do this whenever and wherever you like.

It doesn't really matter whether you felt anything or not when you prayed to receive the Lord and His Spirit. If you believed in your heart that you received, then God's Word promises you did. *"Therefore I say unto you, What things soever ye desire, when ye pray, believe that ye receive* them*, and ye shall have* them*"* (Mark 11:24). God always honors His Word—believe it!

We would like to rejoice with you, pray with you, and answer any questions to help you understand more fully what has taken place in your life!

Please contact us to let us know that you've prayed to be filled with the Holy Spirit and to request the book *The New You & the Holy Spirit*. This book will explain in more detail about the benefits of being filled with the Holy Spirit and speaking in tongues. Call our Helpline: **719-635-1111** (available 24 hours a day, seven days a week).

Call for Prayer

If you need prayer for any reason, you can call our Helpline, 24 hours a day, seven days a week at **719-635-1111**. A trained prayer minister will answer your call and pray with you.

Every day, we receive testimonies of healings and other miracles from our Helpline, and we are ministering God's nearly-too-good-to-be-true message of the Gospel to more people than ever. So, I encourage you to call today!

About the Author

Andrew Wommack's life was forever changed the moment he encountered the supernatural love of God on March 23, 1968. As a renowned Bible teacher and author, Andrew has made it his mission to change the way the world sees God.

Andrew's vision is to go as far and deep with the Gospel as possible. His message goes far through the *Gospel Truth* television program, which is available to over half the world's population. The message goes deep through discipleship at Charis Bible College, headquartered in Woodland Park, Colorado. Founded in 1994, Charis has campuses across the United States and around the globe.

Andrew also has an extensive library of teaching materials in print, audio, and video. More than 200,000 hours of free teachings can be accessed at **awmi.net**.

Contact Information

Andrew Wommack Ministries, Inc.

PO Box 3333
Colorado Springs, CO 80934-3333
info@awmi.net
awmi.net

Helpline: 719-635-1111 (available 24/7)

Charis Bible College

info@charisbiblecollege.org
844-360-9577
CharisBibleCollege.org

For a complete list of all of our offices,
visit **awmi.net/contact-us**.

Connect with us on social media.

Sign up to watch anytime, anywhere, for free.

GOSPEL TRUTH

N E T W O R K

Andrew's
LIVING
COMMENTARY
BIBLE SOFTWARE

Andrew Wommack's *Living Commentary* Bible study software is a user-friendly, downloadable program. It's like reading the Bible with Andrew at your side, sharing his revelation with you verse by verse.

Main features:

- Bible study software with a grace-and-faith perspective
- Over 26,000 notes by Andrew on verses from Genesis through Revelation
- *Matthew Henry's Concise Commentary*
- 12 Bible versions
- 2 concordances: *Englishman's Concordance* and *Strong's Concordance*
- 2 dictionaries: *Collaborative International Dictionary* and *Holman's Dictionary*
- Atlas with biblical maps
- Bible and *Living Commentary* statistics
- Quick navigation, including history of verses
- Robust search capabilities (for the Bible and Andrew's notes)
- "Living" (i.e., constantly updated and expanding)
- Ability to create personal notes

Whether you're new to studying the Bible or a seasoned Bible scholar, you'll gain a deeper revelation of the Word from a grace-and-faith perspective.

Purchase Andrew's *Living Commentary* today at **awmi.net/living**, and grow in the Word with Andrew.

Item code: 8350

ANDREW WOMMACK
MINISTRIES

CHARIS
BIBLE COLLEGE

God has **more** for you.

Are you longing to find your God-given purpose? At Charis Bible College you will establish a firm foundation in the Word of God and receive hands-on ministry experience to **find, follow,** and **fulfill** your purpose.

Scan the QR code for a free Charis teaching!

CharisBibleCollege.org
Admissions@awmcharis.com
(844) 360-9577

Change your life. **Change the world.**